Renovating Madness

© Copyright 2018 Karen Knight and Liz McQuilkin

All poems included here are copyright to the authors and no copies may be made in any manner whatsoever without first gaining written permission through the publisher.

> Walleah Press
> PO Box 368
> North Hobart
> Tasmania 7002 Australia
> ralph.wessman@walleahpress.com.au

Cover image: © Liz McQuilkin

ISBN: 9781877010415

Renovating Madness

Poems of Willow Court and the Royal Derwent Hospital,
New Norfolk, Tasmania

Karen Knight and Liz McQuilkin

Foreword

When I started work as a clinical and community psychologist in the 1970s, the Royal Derwent Hospital at New Norfolk accommodated close to a thousand residents: elderly people with dementia, people with alcohol and drug dependency, those with long-term or acute short-term mental illness, forensic patients, people with intellectual disability, and those who had simply lived there most of their lives, the original reasons for their admission long forgotten.

The complex was regarded as progressive and quite modern. Within its boundaries, there was everything patients needed: occupational therapy and industrial therapy, a school, a theatre, and a swimming pool. There were hairdressers, cobblers and a tailor. Many staff lived on site, with the doctors' houses and gardens along the well-kept roads. The nurses' home, heated summer and winter by the boiler, towered in the grounds. It was a self-contained little town, within the small town of New Norfolk.

Over the years, imagine the myriad experiences and histories, think of the stories each person could tell, every resident and every staff member ....

This wonderful collection of poetry captures some of those stories from the early days through to the closure of the complex in 2001. The poems are organised thematically rather than historically, as poets Liz McQuilkin and Karen Knight tell about the buildings, the treatments, the experience of parents, about absconding and freedom, about Christmas celebrations, about attachment, belonging and decay.

People with mental illness or intellectual disability are no longer cared for in these large institutions: the new wisdom of community care was beginning in the 1970s and saw wards progressively close from the 1980s as smaller long-term facilities opened and acute care was managed through general hospitals.

This collection compels us to reflect on the extraordinary power and influence of the institution over so many individuals for so many years. And we wonder whether this was, on balance, a good or a bad way of caring for people. And perhaps we conclude – as always in a complex world – that it was both.

>   Mary Blackwood
>   Former State Manager, Mental Health Services,
>   Tasmania

Contents

We see the distant past (LM)	1
What's in a name? (LM)	2
Atonement (KK)	3
Arthur's conscience (LM)	4
The grand façade (KK)	5
Thirteen reasons for admission (KK)	6
Homeless in a home (LM)	7
Sorrow (KK)	8
Millbrook Rise Psychopathic Hospital (LM)	9
Parent pain (LM)	10
Six cures (KK)	11
Overcrowded (LM)	13
Unfit for duty (LM)	15
Committed (LM)	17
Keeper H informs the doctor (LM)	18
Alonnah (KK)	19
Endurance (KK)	20
Hot bath and blanket treatment (LM)	21
Mystery chair (LM)	22
The blacksmith and his weathervane (LM)	23
Emus and others in residence (LM)	24
My mother remembers (LM)	25
In the hospital grounds (KK)	26
Devotion (LM)	27
Shell-shocked (LM)	28
The ugly word (LM)	29
For life (LM)	31

Wanted (KK)	32
Asylum fashions (LM)	33
Entanglement (KK)	34
Shelf-help (KK)	35
Custom-made (LM)	36
Outing (KK)	37
Roll up, roll up … (KK)	38
Dairy joy (KK)	40
The escape plan (KK)	41
Release (KK)	42
The art of breaking free (KK)	43
Absconder (LM)	44
The incurable (KK)	45
Missing (KK)	46
Town alert (LM)	47
Beyond blue (KK)	48
Gossip (KK)	49
Soberland (KK)	50
For a song (KK)	51
Prescription (KK)	52
Metamorphosis (LM)	53
Demolition (LM)	54
Unearthing (KK)	55
Mess of potage (LM)	56
Mary-Anne's story (LM)	57
Young teacher-in-charge (LM)	58
Christmas Eve (LM)	60
Remaining residents (LM)	62
Last dance at Lyprenny (LM)	63
Belonging (LM)	64
Deinstitutionalization (LM)	65
Ward 12 (KK)	66

Casualties (KK)	67
The ha-ha wall (LM)	69
Convict wall (LM)	71
The garden (KK)	72
Renovating madness (KK)	73
Shattered (KK)	74
Glass breakers (KK)	75
Xmas (KK)	76
The beauty of numbers (KK)	77
Statistics (LM)	78
Why graffiti? (KK)	79
Seven ages (LM)	81
New Norfolk (LM)	82
Catharsis (LM)	83
Timeline	84
Bibliography	86

For Emerald, with admiration and deep affection
　　　　　　　　　　　　　　　　　　　Karen

For Megan, dear friend and mentor
　　　　　　　　　　　　　Liz

We see the distant past
through dusty windows
covered in cobwebs
and rampant blackberries
a world gripped by stigma
misconceptions, fears.

We see the recent past
through shattered glass
where waves of vandals
have violently conquered
a place and a time
the world is keen to forget.

What's in a name?

New Norfolk 1833 – 2001
(Found poem)

Invalid Barracks
Colonial Hospital
Madhouse
Her Majesty's Lunatic Asylum
Hospital for the Insane
Nut Factory
Mental Diseases Hospital
Loony Bin
Lachlan Park Hospital
Millbrook Rise
Funny Farm
Royal Derwent Hospital
Willow Court Training Centre.

Atonement

This clutch of buildings
has long died
but the ghosts are still here
trying to find heartbeats.

We need to lie
the mirrors down
and take a hammer
to them.

Make a mandala
out of all this
crazed glass.

This place needs
blessing
before the ghosts reach
breaking point.

We need to mend.

Arthur's conscience

Governor's Retreat, New Norfolk, May 1827

Making decisions in Hobarton – all very well
but ailing convict numbers are causing chaos.
Why decree they all be sent up here
to the Invalid Depot?
                               You didn't think it through.

Look at the miserable state of these new arrivals.
Three nights in an open boat in driving rain.
This morning, fog – a *jerry* the men call it –
 they couldn't sail till midday.
                                   Pity the wretches:

infection, malnutrition, chronic rheumatics.
At least a cart is ready to convey them
to the old depot. God only help them there:
every part of it leaks.
                                 Do something, Arthur.

Use the authority England has given you:
requisition clothing, blankets, beds.
Write home today for funds, and order plans
for a new invalid barracks.
                                      No time to lose.

The Grand Façade

From Peppermint Hill lookout
the large-scale asylum
is a postcode unto itself
with buildings sprawled out
like a row of birds in full flight
their staggered wings modelled
to chase down the sun
and spread the mind's greening.

Through the louvred windows
light brings the landscape inside.
Trees shake their crowns
blossom colours the walls.
A cross-wind blows
into the mouths of the mad —
light drills into their bones.

Building designs that increased natural day-lighting, used colour and texture, encouraged movement and incorporated nature, were once thought to improve mental health amongst incarcerated patients. After further investigation, this was proved wrong.

Thirteen reasons for admission

1864 - 1889
(Found poem)

Bloody flux
Death of sons in war
Dissipation of nerves
Hysteria
Ill treatment by husband
Imaginary female trouble
Menstrual deranged
Medicine to prevent conception
Novel reading
Nymphomania
Parents were cousins
Scarlatina
Time of life

Homeless in a home

A child of the fifties
I could have been one of them:
born with cerebral palsy
Down Syndrome
or anything that hindered
growing up *normal*.
Plucked from my family,
banished to Lachlan Park
a hundred miles from home.

Admitted
to a crowded dormitory.
Day and night in my cot
tied down with bandages
if deemed out of control.
Out-of-sight out-of-mind child
in a world detached from tears.

All seasons, no seasons
a ghetto of stunned air
imperative voice of nurse
the bruising shout of power.
Wheeled outside, rarely,
to a patch of grass called playground.
No toys, no clothes of my own
innocent of love –
alive but not living.

Sorrow

A homeless cat shrinks
beneath a man fern.
His coat stares after the rain.

The S.A.D. girl sniffs the life
from a bell-shaped flower
her daily rush of blue.

Along the path, a snail shies away
from groundsmen
in Blundstone boots.

Far from the ward's pallor
a nurse wheels an epileptic
into the last blade of sunshine.

S.A.D. — Seasonal Affective Disorder

Millbrook Rise Psychopathic Hospital

1935

Cream, Art Deco, it looks like a country club
with lawns, shrubs, tennis court, croquet green –
A home away from home, the brochure says.

Veterans of World War I
and private paying patients
persuaded to come for rest-cures

breathe the fresh country air
sample the latest drugs
engage in electric and hydro therapies.

Above the door, a plaque – *The Rising Sun* –
symbol of hope and remembrance.

Curtains are carefree-bright
but blinds are drawn
like half-closed eyes.

Wooden beams and panelled walls
darken reception rooms.
Armchairs recline as if medicated.

Alone in the smokers' room
a patient awaits new treatment
fear in his eyes.

How still the air
how silent the passageways.

Parent pain

c1950s

They don't talk about their visits
to a place called Millbrook Rise
the stigma too hard to bear.

They confine the facts to family
and a few close friends.
They don't talk about their visits

better to confine their son
when he has an episode
the stigma too hard to bear.

They know the signs:
his mood suddenly plummets.
They don't talk about their visits,

when delusions take over
they bundle him into the car
the stigma too hard to bear.

When the demons within cry out:
The Commies are coming to get me
they don't talk about their visits
the stigma too hard to bear.

Six cures

18th to mid 20th century treatments

Historically, people looked upon mental illness as something other than illness, and attempted to eliminate the problem in horrific ways that not only did not cure or help the sufferers, but likely traumatised them even more.

Trepanation

Drill holes into the skull so that evil spirits can escape. What better way to rid the patient of these trapped demons than by giving them a way out. Sorry, no anaesthetic has been invented yet.

Hydrotherapy

Strip the patient and wrap him like an Egyptian mummy, using towels soaked in iced water. Restrain in a tub for days at a time, allowing only for short bathroom breaks. If this doesn't cure him of religious excitement, bind him in a crucifix position and turn a fire hose on him.

How to remove extra emotions

Render the patient unconscious via an electric shock. The new, improved ice-pick-through-the-eye-socket method takes only ten minutes to access the brain and cut out a piece of tissue.

Hysteria therapy for women

Calm the wayward uterus by having the patient breathe in noxious fumes. Get the uterus settled in doing what it is there for. Women need to get married and start having babies. Guaranteed to cure nervousness, fainting and reading too many novels.

Rotational Therapy

Do what Darwin's grandfather believed in. Spin the patient around very fast on a chair-like device suspended by chains from the ceiling. This reduces brain congestion, curing the mental disorder and inducing sleep. Side effects include dizziness.

Lobotomy

The old time favourite. Cut away the frontal lobe of a violent, faeces-throwing monkey and watch how it becomes docile. For doctors willing to take to the road in their lobotomobiles and provide treatment onsite to anyone who is keen – from sunstroke sufferers to bored housewives. It's a real Nobel Prize winner.

Overcrowded

Invalid Barracks, New Norfolk, 1848

*All capable men to be moved
to Impression Bay Probation Station.
Be ready to leave at first light.
Refuse, and you fend for yourselves
beyond locked gates.*

Thirteen years I bin sharin
wiv convicts and duffers.
I will not leave.

Impression Bay.
Hellhole I calls it:
prisoners sick wiv fevers
maimed or graveyard old
all forced to work.

I served the fourteen year
and earnt me freedom
at nearby Saltwater River
minin and cartin coal.

Impression Bay:
the name chills me blood
triggers the throbbin of me scars
from them brutish leg-irons
drives me near to madness.

I hears me name: *William Cardwell*.
Send me back? I be eighty-seven,
lame. And blind.

Yet capable, say the officer
able to reason.
Only the lunatics stay.

A cruel word, *lunatic.*
I know each one by 'is voice and touch.
Me helpers, me eyes. Good duffers —
they sun me days.
I will not leave.

But reason say: Old man
ye cannot rail agin the order.
How could ye survive
eyeless, beyond the gates?

Be ready wiv bowl and blanket.
Go where they send thee.

Unfit for duty

H.M. Gaol, Hobart, 1894

Have ya heard? Poor John Leary
is dead.

We missed 'im at the gaol.
One of us 'e was, one o' the best.
Heaven knows a warder's life ain't easy
and work with loony criminals
that's the worst.
But John, 'e had a softy's heart –
'e cared for them crazy creatures.

When that ward were closed
the inmates carted off to the asylum
'e said 'e had to go –
couldn' refuse promotion
what with fam'ly to feed
and jobs bein' hard to find.
But we all knew
'e wouldn' leave those men.

Then the flu strikes.
Consumption sets in.
The story goes, the Superintendent
give 'im a month's paid leave –
whoever heard o' that?

From the time 'e first spit blood
John never miss a day –
6 till 6, one Sunday off in three.
Criminal hours.

Eight months on
'e asks for two days off
then back to work another month —
coughin', wastin' away
finally told: *Unfit for Duty.*

Three days later, poor John Leary
'e was dead.

Committed

Ladies' Cottage, New Norfolk.
April 12th, 1875

Dear Husband,

Let me come home.
It has been three years
since I held my baby.
 'Post-partum depression,' the doctor said
'a new term for an old affliction.'
As if I did not know my Latin —
we use it here for private messages.
Remember how my cloud of sadness lifted
six months after each confinement?
Have you so easily forgotten
how it was when Michael and James were born?
Do they remember me?
Does our little daughter thrive?
I miss them so.
Rumour is rife:
a man may have his wife committed
if he tires of her.
The nurses declare it is easy:
a doctor to sign a paper
money to pay the hospital.
It has been three years
since I saw my children.
Husband, let me come home.

Your Dutiful Wife

Keeper H informs the doctor

Gentlemen's Cottage, 1883

It's Wardsman B again.
He's shut Mr T in the black hole
for refusing to be his lackey.

He's mocked the new arrival
the young toff, Mr G,
and whipped him with his belt.

They say he fakes the files,
pretending he's handed out
all the medicines.

He gives himself airs, yet steals
the gentlemen's special comforts –
brandy, porter, wine.

Come quick and look you, Sir.
He's wearing patients' clothing
and smoking their tobacco.

Now he's drunk on duty
and sleeping. Pinned to his vest
a note: *Do not disturb.*

He demands a skivvy wake him
ahead of your hospital rounds.
Come, Sir. Afore he stirs.

Alonnah

Female Security Ward

Zelda sang bloody murder
in the shower block.
Her voice ripped through
the curtain rings.

Patricia missed her books
on drowning, shooting, gassing.
She found them more dazzling
than Mills & Boon.

Dorothy swept the ward
with a fine-tooth comb
in search of keys
to the liquor cupboard.

She never found the keys
because there were none –
and there never was
a liquor cupboard.

Endurance

In the communal bathroom
after morning showers
a half-drowned flea
in need of a warm body
figure-skates the linoleum floor
scales a glacier of ceramic tiles
Evel Knievels over three toilets
two baths and a line of basins
to find a fresh host.

Hot bath and blanket treatment

1847

… *a seething bath, which yet men prove*
against strange maladies a sovereign cure.
                    Shakespeare, Sonnet 153

Thomas, at twenty-four,
is abandoned by family.
They judge and label him:
not quite right.

A little financial inducement
finds a cleric who fills in forms.
Thomas is sent to the asylum
on a verdict of madness.

Less than three months later
his mother doesn't know him:
blonde curls cut off,
the shaved head ages him.

His demand for release
offends some of the warders.
Peevishly, they deal out
punishment:

secure him with canvas straps
in a scalding metal bath,
a blanket around his head
blocking out light.

They leave him   seven hours
calling, bawling, for help.
Abandoned at twenty-four
Thomas is pulled out – dead.

Mystery chair

2004

In one of the upper rooms
crusted with dust and droppings
a chair on stilts.
Above it, remains of a frame.

A stage prop?

A canopied throne for King Lear
before he went mad and wandered
into wilderness?

Or a treatment chair?

Not the whirling one on wires
where patients were spun
until calmed.

Perhaps an Oldmissbunny
with her cruel contraption of clamps
for immobilising limbs –
but there's no sign of those.

Rather, a Bergonic precursor
for electric shocks –
yet the structure wouldn't cope
with seizures.

Maybe a Tranquilising Chair
with soft leather straps (since removed)
the patients hidden from view
behind hessian – note the remnant.

The blacksmith and his weathervane

The clock-tower of Refractory Ward K1
1889

For steeples and towers
he always made rooster vanes
to herald a new dawn – and hope.

This one is different: a swallow
with arrowed head and outstretched neck
a forked tail upright to catch the wind

spinning, seeming to fly, but fixed
by a shaft with straitjacket grip –
like the inmates, a tethered unravelling.

From narrow Gothic windows
do they see his metal bird
outlined against the moon?

Do they note the wind changes?

Emus and others in residence

c1912

It's part of a plan the hospital has embraced
to provide pleasant surroundings: a new form
of therapy, the power of nature to heal.

Flightless, the emus roam within the walls.
Sometimes they emit a drumming sound
but mostly they merely grunt.

Not like those two rogue peacocks.
What a racket they make. No-one knows
where they came from — they simply flew in.

The guards at the gate feed and encourage them
to stay, for everyone knows those raucous calls
can drown the cries of patients.

My mother remembers

At the home of Superintendent Dr GE Aitken
1931

One of the gardeners thought
he was Napoleon.
He strutted about, boasting
of victories and strategies.
Asked how Josephine fared,
he pointed to a rose
saying, *See for yourself.*

Another believed
he was God.
He planted, watered, weeded,
resurrected,
swept the paths, kept things neat,
lent on his broom and surveyed
the realm of His Garden –
His Creation.

LM's mother lived with the Superintendent's family during her time as infant mistress at New Norfolk School (1931 – 33).

In the Hospital Grounds

Big city Mafiosi
would have been more discreet
clean cut across the throat
while the security guard slept
but not for this Russian Blue tom
with tortured grin, half-skinned
by savagery.

This time tomorrow
ads will appear in the
Lost and Founds
photos will be taped
on shop-front windows
and when the tins of gourmet
are past their use-by-date
cat shows and breeders
will be visited, till the owner
finds a clone.

Now, on the hospital grounds
the postman is out of step
the charge nurse covers her eyes
as the greenkeeper takes up a shovel
and a swarm of wasps thanks the tom
for what they have already received.

Devotion

1919

In a ward set aside
for patients with Spanish Flu
Sub-matron (Miss) EL Davies
ministers with patience,
calms confused minds.

She glides between iron bedsteads
soothing with voice and touch.
Her starched uniform rustles
like windswept leaves on frost.
Slow night turns and twists.

A dark silence engulfs
barred windows, as clouds
blanket a waning moon.
By dawn another will die
calling out for her.

Steeped in September fog
the hospital wakes to news:
Sub-matron (Miss) EL Davies
of twenty-three years service
succumbed to Spanish Flu.

Shell-shocked

2017

Anxious to tell his story
a local waylays a tourist
outside Esperance Ward:

*They put 'em here
and threw away the key.*

He tells her of uniformed veterans
within the asylum grounds
marching day after day

unable to shed memories
of comrades blown to pieces
or buried alive by shell-burst

forever entrenched, hearing
the deadly rattle of machine guns
the endless thunder of the big guns

scraping imagined mud
from battered boots and gaiters

convinced they were still at war.

The ugly word

Tell me of Gallipoli.
I'll tell of battles raging
decades after The Armistice:
insidious war played out
not on beaches or in trenches
but in homes, in everyday lives.

Tell me of brutal acts
in fields ravaged by cannon fire
in villages bombed to oblivion.
I'll tell of love turned sour
in households besieged by shame.

Syphilis hisses menace.

Its venomous breath struck fear
as it spread and sped across Europe
pronouncing death or servitude
upon returning soldiers and their wives,
nurses, sweethearts,
unborn children.

Tell me of comradeship, courage.
I'll tell of suffering, blame,
soldiers afflicted, committed –
Paralysis of the Insane –
wives infected, not knowing
they carried this monstrous disease.

Tell me stories of heroes.
I'll tell of damaged infants —
blind, deaf, deformed —
hidden behind closed doors
or banished to oblivion —
to the asylum.

For life

Carlton Ward for the criminally insane, c1950

Each morning I begin by walking
        What else can he do? We insist on exercise.
close to the wall with its overhanging curve.
        We give him half an hour to stretch his legs.
Then I stand in the yard's centre, below a field of sky
        You can hear him mumbling, sometimes calling out.
and watch the saddles and slow rises
        We take no notice unless he disturbs others.
of hills moving around the horizon
        No talking, we say, but he doesn't heed our words.
speaking their gentle urgings
        He needs to be here, in high security.
and grief – like the albatross – slips from my neck.
        Time to move him back to his cell.
The kindly sun anoints me. Lord, have mercy –
        Did I hear him just now say albatross?

WANTED

A smart, respectable woman
modest in demeanour
skilled in the art of plain cooking
a good worker at her needle
desires the acquaintance
of a respectable, refined
older gentleman
with a charitable disposition
to escort her
out of these disabled doors
these psychiatric windows
away from all chemical restraints
and the lack of human kindness.

Asylum fashions

Why not slip on this jacket, check if it fits?
It's just arrived from England. You're the first
to sample it. We've had just a few old ones
until today – we don't use them much.

Let's see you put it on. Yes, I know
the sleeves are long, the end cloths well beyond
your finger tips – this is the latest style.
Note the firmness of fabric. It's ever so strong.

Now for the matching trousers. Like to try them?
I'll hold the waist open while you step inside.
The centre seam that stitches the legs together
is well thought-out and perfectly discreet.

The outfit is complete with these two mittens.
The same tight weave, and with a novel feature
of metal clasp and lock, defining the wrist –
an elegant innovation, practical too.

Let's leave the mittens for now. See how the jacket
keeps you snug when I tie the sleeves around you.
No more hugging yourself against the cold –
this latest model neatly does the trick.

Entanglement

The sea has washed up a swarm
of translucent jellyfish.

She wants her hands back
to scoop up the soft shapes,
set them adrift again.

Her upper body is numb
as blood pools into her elbows –
the swelling has begun.

They have made the straitjacket
too tight again, but she insists on
walking the full length of the beach.

As her bones and muscles stiffen
she counts the gelatinous bells
and trailing tentacles of the jellyfish –

as if she is witnessing
a rarity.

Shelf-help

Staying on the Moonsick Path
that old familiar gown.

Brainsick Anonymous
the brain fog fix.

How to Attract the Mondo Bizarre
be yourself.

The Unhinged Guide to Great Sex
flirting with madness.

Draw your Way to a Better Mind
for non-linear eyes only.

Secrets about Life all Lifers should Know
protect yourself from others.

Meditations for Those who Feel too Much
pre-meditated meditation.

Natural Born Misfits
born-again misfits.

Rewire your Anxious Self
reach down the rabbit hole.

The Power of the Certifiable
achieving mental health.

Custom-made

No longer that heavy tread
of the mass-produced

Agnes walks on air
in new boots
of rich brown leather
with a bright green strap –
made at the hospital
solely for her.

A nurse
gentles her into them
fastens the brass locks
pockets the key:

These boots kept on
will protect your feet
from the cold.

Locked in for the day
Agnes walks them
runs and skips.

Flashes of bright green
unleash her happiness

each strap
with its line of dainty holes
each catch
a golden jewel at her ankle.

Outing

Dennes Point, Bruny Island, early 1960s

Henry counted each step
from bus to beach
then lunged into the sea
and danced back out again
leaving the waves to clean up
after his untidy body
left a ring around the tide.

Gathering up gifts
of sea eggs, tiny skulls
and shells to decorate
the window ledge
of his barren ward,

he turned his back
on sandpiper tracks
and polka-dot bikinis
life-buoys and shipwrecks
and a washed up whale.

Henry counted each step
back from beach to bus
his beach bag bursting
with souvenirs.

Roll up, roll up...

Lennon Brothers Circus, The Esplanade, January, 1977

(i)

The big top
striped black and gold
like a giant performing cat
stretches its jaws
gulps down fences
rolls above rooftops
meets at eye level
the tips of historic poplar trees
till the flag of clowns
flies and tickles the sky
and the sky
doesn't seem to mind.

(ii)

Pysch-ward carers
lead the low-risk lodgers
past brazen costumes
and roaring music, to catch
a close-up of three caged lions
with desert-tinged manes
sniffing a transitory breeze.

What joy
to be on the outside
looking in.

All afternoon,
the lodgers marvel
at the big cats —
with their honeystone heads
and wild animal breath —
licking the bars
of their Bastille.

Dairy joy

Behind the empty mortuary
a red and white striped ice-cream shop
has popped up overnight.
The sign above the door says:
DREAMSICLES

a temptation from this rough
and tumble world to sample
the premium dream coolness
of butterfat flavours
all hand-made from scratch.

From Alcheringa House
in a serpentine queue, children
are fidgety in their autistic skins
waiting to taste the better side
of glorious

to hold the soft texture
of a creamy swirl in a cone
Happy Happy Joy Joys
Crazy Charlie Sundaes
Brain Freeze Lemon Sorbets.

Against the Modesty Wall
naughty girls from A Ward
burn daylight, fabricating
Bittersweet Mint, Death by Chocolate
Frost Bite Fudgecide.

The escape plan

One afternoon
we will find
that deserted street.

The reels of film
extinguished
the showdown shotguns
shoved
in the torn-off trash cans.

The automobile
will be tethered
to a street lamp
humming horsepower.

And we'll ride off
together
into the sunset.

Release

A round bird-mirror
with chain and bell
hangs from the rusty iron
slide bolt of a heavy
Tasmanian Oak door
labelled RS34
a reference perhaps
to a key to set free
a caged warm-blooded
inmate
with the ability
to fly.

The art of breaking free

Find an open shed
star-high with tools
and a golden ladder
that will reach the top
of a maximum security wall.

As you climb each rung
don't listen to the bricks
and their sad history
the willow trees are waiting
for you on the other side.

When you cross
the bridge
don't look down
at the troubled river

don't dwell on
the lifers
you leave behind.

Absconder

What he wants
is space for solitude –
an unbroken view
of valleys and hills
a stream of running water
to quench thirst and sadness.

What he wants
is to eat when he's hungry
smoke if he feels the need
read without interruption
choose where and when
to sleep, to dream.

What he wants
is what's left of life
back in his control
that's why he's run away
from the charge of madness
the sentence of captivity.

The Incurable

The night she got out
they crossed themselves.
No-one thought
of a double-check head count.

All the doors were locked
with the one master key
but she still took the nurses
by surprise,

catching them off guard
with her revenge dagger.

She was found rocking
the ward's baby doll,
her newborn angel
she had come to reclaim –

hair, so human,
eyelashes lush,
silicone vinyl
soft, gentle touch

saliva at the corner
of its mouth

and the veins
so real.

Missing

Like a man
with a metal detector
he fossicks
through the rubble
of crumbling walls
and stone
in search
of his memory
gone astray
after the asylum
he once lived in
tumbled down.

Town alert

There it goes: the siren's wail.
The town stops and counts the blasts:
three of them, each ten seconds long
a dangerous patient is on the loose.

The rasping bellows reach the hills
echo up and down the valley
wage their war in leafless poplars
swell across the still river.

Doors are bolted, windows checked.
Sounds are heightened, time sits heavy.
Thick fog settles, blankets houses.
Silence shifts on restless feet.

Beyond Blue

Freed from all things
earthbound

the touched ones
in institutional shrouds

hover
with their cloud throwers

filling the gaps between
sky and low ragged mist

surrounding themselves
in cumulus bliss.

Gossip

He, a health care worker
had blue-printed the weekend skillfully.
French letters, multi-coloured,
purchased in a bold sweat

the caravan park paid
in advance
and a copy of *Lady Chatterley's Lover*
to be read aloud while plaiting her hair.

She, a nurses' aide
had rehearsed the perfect alibi
left her husband a crock-pot
of his favourite stew

finished work early
to buy a pink negligee
and bottles of wine
to strengthen the nerve.

Their co-workers said it would never come off.

A last-minute change in the shifts
and miniature balloons, multi-coloured
took French leave from the Day Room window
and exploded in the heat.

Soberland

High functioning addicts
are getting used to the dry rush
of a liquor-free lifestyle
now their moonshine days
are behind them.

They're learning to walk
the night-cart shift
through liver-cleansing streets
where blood lights shine
and never black out
and they get to see sunrise
now they're up with the parting
of hospital curtains.

This morning one of them
out for a spin in a V8 elixir
rolled her tongue over
a milk thistle tonic.
Her body was haloed
in a bright carrot glow.

The doctors are keeping
the word *broken*
from her beautiful bones.

A number of alcoholics and drug addicts in the 1960s and 70s admitted themselves voluntarily to the Royal Derwent Hospital because they wanted sobriety. Some were there to get out of repeated drunk driving charges and jail, only to reoffend once they were discharged.

For a song

He rowed his alabaster dinghy
to the nearest wine bar
where he wallowed in habit
with other worn-down drinkers.

Weathered by untipped cigarettes
booze and sadness, he swayed
to the tune of Sinatra's larynx
*One for my Baby and one more
for the Road.*

When the money ran out
his mind slipped its moorings.

He sold his alabaster dinghy
for two fingers of Jack Daniels
three ice cubes and
a splash of water.

Prescription

Sing
in the tropical rain
of your illness
turn it inside out
like a difficult
umbrella.
        Kick
        the head of it
        into gutters
        splash
        around in
        the pain.
                Lean
                into a streetlight
                and read
                a storm of poems
                that would pale
                a bolt of lightning.
                        Empty
                        the pressure cooker
                        of all doctors
                        prescriptions
                        and psychotropic
                        drugs.
                                Your
                                bounce-back-ability
                                will
                                return.
                                I promise.

Metamorphosis

1960s

Down the hill from weeping Willow Court
over a bridge across the Lachlan
up a gentle slope. You've left
the nineteenth century well behind
entered the twentieth half way through —
the Royal Derwent set out like a town.

No more institution-gloom
of colonial stone or Victorian brick
but modern, airy bungalows
each a separate entity
spread across an open field:
admissions, wards, chapel and nurses' home.

With medications now the new restraint
Asylum has morphed into *Hospital*.

Demolition

K1 Ward, 1965

The old order changeth, yielding place to new,
And God fulfils himself in many ways,
Lest one good custom should corrupt the world.
                    Tennyson, Morte D'Arthur

The explosion was deafening.
The clock-tower resisted, barely shook.
The second attempt succeeded.

Base in bits, it toppled almost intact
dignified, right to the end
when the ground reached up and shattered it.

A wall of dust rose in a soft grey shroud,
billowed and dispersed.
Eyes smarted. Heads turned away.

The town lost its landmark
the hospital its focal point
the patients a familiar face.

Unearthing

Beneath the rotting floorboards
a mob of sheep are bleating
Butchery on our bones
prime lamb cuts missing.

A mob of sheep are bleating
Fatty meat for mutes
prime lamb cuts missing.
Excavators edgy.

Fatty meat for mutes
shame on puffed-up gentry.
Excavators edgy
lanolin clouds rising.

Shame on puffed-up gentry
butchery on our bones.
Lanolin clouds rising
beneath the rotting floorboards.

In 2017, during excavations below Room 12 at The Barracks, a sizeable cache of butchered animal bones, mainly from sheep, was uncovered under the floorboards. Very few bones of hind limbs were recovered. One might assume that patients staying in the main part of the Barracks were fed low quality meat, while the better cuts were given to higher-status patients.

Mess of potage

Here they come, each with her metal bowl.
Dole out the broth, a ladle for each woman.
Don't waste time smiling, making conversation –
they're strangers to pleasantries.

No point in turning your nose up at the soup.
They like it just as it is. Fills their bellies.
Easy to make: off-cuts of fatty mutton
boiled up with bones until the gristle softens
and the ribs give up their secrets.

Plenty of barley to thicken, there's nothing else.
You can tell this skilly hasn't been boiled enough:
the grains are still hard, no decent consistency.
Did you take out all the bones, just as I told you?
These inmates will swallow the lot.

Not much flavour here: no herbs or praties.
Put in more salt and give the pail a stir.
Remember their piece of meat, one ration, no more
or they'll fight for it, fist and claw.

Mary-Anne's story

Tasmania, 1930

She wouldn't have known
this holding of rich land
which fed the cattle and grew the crops
this family farm of fifty years
would be the source of her bane.

She wouldn't have known
heavy rainfall on this steep terrain
leached out iodine from the soil
forging the doom though not the death
of her unborn child.

She couldn't have known
for no-one knew back then
why her baby was born deaf
front of the skull enlarged
slow tongue protruding.

She would have known
the fear on every face
of every other mother
the town poised to whisper
idiot, halfwit, cretin.

She would have known
what everyone expected
as soon as the child was weaned:
take her by train to New Norfolk
and leave her there.

Young teacher-in-charge

Margaret Reynolds at Lachlan Park Special School, 1963

(i)

She holds fast the master key
as guards wave her through iron gates
set in wire-topped concrete walls.

She enters institution-brick,
roofs caught in a sombre sky
windows barred and sightless.

Chosen by nurses, the sixteen children
arrive at a converted ward.
What of the others?

Unteachable. The word bombards her.

The children are mute – by nature or choice?
She can't decipher the vacant looks.

She sings to them, dances, acts the clown –
anything for a flicker of response.
Eyes brighten, minds engage with music:

the smallest smiles appear
mouths begin to shape a word
hands locate each other and clap.

(ii)

She watches as nurses deliver her charges
on mobile beds, in wheelchairs, or walking
with purpose, knowing the way.

Some come close and stroke her arm
heads nestle against her neck.
She's learned to expect this open affection.

Why not return it?
Explore the message touch can bring?
Teacher training never taught her that.

The children arrive in larger numbers.
Staff are recruited, classrooms created
equipment in truckloads donated.

(iii)

She targets the teenage boys: delinquents
longing for a world outside the walls.
They swarm over her daily paper

point at pictures, pore over captions
desperate to read. No more beatings:
they'd rather be in school.

She's changing the culture.
No-one is unteachable, she says.
Faces flush with learning.

Christmas Eve

Morning

A busy day ahead for the man in red —
visiting patients, shaking hands.

He leaves the best till last
the children's wards:

hands out lucky dips
to boys and girls in the dayrooms

to toddlers and teens
confined in cots

bottle-feeds the babies
hums them *Silent Night*.

Afternoon

A boy in a wheelchair
crests the wave of *Jingle Bells*
singing in jangles of sounds.

He dances wasted arms
his lifeless legs beneath a rug
of red and green.

Yuletide colours, a nurse declares
wheeling the tablet trolley
out of sight.

The boy is transfixed by a large red bell
its honeycomb tissue opened out
to a perfect shape.

He carols the bell
immersing himself
in the blessing of being.

Evening

They arrive at the hall early
in wheelchairs decked with balloons
or walking awkwardly in fancy dress –

angels draped in hospital sheets
wise men in turbans, shepherds in tea-towels
a walking-talking Christmas tree –

the rest in their best.

Matron sweeps in with military splendour:
signals the band. They strike up *Deck the halls*.
The parade shuffles forward.

'Tis the season to be jolly

till it's time to return to the wards.
In the foyer, they gather round the manger
singing *Jingle Bells,* over and over

while the man in red shakes every hand
calls every guest his *Heavenly Host*.

Remaining residents

June, 2000

There's pride in the hospital grounds.
The gardening team are sweeping
armfuls of late autumn into bins.
I'm a leaf picker-upper, says one.
Lived here all my life, another.
A third mouths his elusive words
to a whispering, teasing wind.

There's pride by the concrete wall
of a former exercise yard.
Four are shovelling sawdust into bags:
I get my workout here, says one.
Get paid 25 a week, another.
The tongue-tied pair affirm with nods
under a changing sky.

There's pride in the furniture workshop.
Head to head, two are constructing a table.
Others sit watching and drinking tea
except a very old man, absorbed
in snipping buttons from cast-off clothes
and a very young man rocking back and forth –
accepted, included, calm.

There's pride in the women's craftroom:
*I work here Mondey Tuesdey Wensdey
Thursdey   Fridey,* says one triumphantly.
Used to pack pegs, another.
Before the factory closed, a third.
The basket weavers and bonbon makers
silenced by concentration.

Last dance in Lyprenny

September, 2000

The dayroom fills with music.
A strobe dispenses colours on dancing couples
and patients standing alone, sidelined by shyness,
steeped in rhythms of the town's local band.

There's dignity in the duo taking the floor:
he does his best to dodge her little feet,
her left hand firmly clutches his right shoulder,
his right cautiously, lightly, touches her waist.

They do not talk, a hand held is enough.
If they could, they might say:
*Home was once a distant place
but home is now and here.* They might say that.

Tomorrow he'll be outside, mowing, weeding,
working under a watchful, discreet eye.
She'll be inside, wrapping Christmas bonbons
for a world she barely knows beyond the gates.

Lyprenny, a ward for patients with intellectual disability, was closed a few weeks later.

Belonging

I like being here
with English trees
grazing cattle
hills I can almost touch
whopping skies
I can't.

I like the routines
of meals
walking the ward
basket-weaving
time to rise
time to sleep.

I like my friends
most of the nurses
my doctor
the cleaners.

I'm safe here —
it's where I belong.

Deinstitutionalization

2001

Say it slowly
to savour the meaning:
de-in-sti-tu-tion-al-iz-a-tion.
No more segregation —
the buzz word is integration.

Blending new wisdom
with good old-fashioned pragmatism,
our government has closed the hospital,
moved doctors, nurses and inmates
into the city.

No more open spaces,
fresh air, sunshine, trees.
Here, patients are bound
in a single, one-for-all jacket
of high-rise concrete and glass.

Ward 12

A stray kitten
the colour of terra-cotta
is perfecting her armour-plating
as she negotiates floors
of fractured glass.

She is compelled to play
this Russian Roulette
now she has come to recognise
the smell of tinned cat food
and the sound of water flowing
into a willow-patterned bowl.

Twice a day a former nurse
with a flair for kindness
sweeps the entrance
and sets down food
away from the thicket
of neglect.

Casualties

Squatting in the bitumen
by the old mortuary
suckering weeds
of blackberry.

Around the hem
of the exercise yard
runtish holly.

Under the scum and stench
of the Frascati pond
rotting water ribbons
and frogs.

An ash sapling
tunnelling too far
is trapped in the pipeline.

Wisteria and ivy
in a race to the high wall
have growth-spurted
through the fire escape.

A solitary elm
scrooches down
in the empty avenue.

Lombardy pine
has surrendered
its heartwood
to a colony of bees.

A laurel has died
but the earth holds fast
its mouldering roots.

The golden robinia
has lost its vitals —
creamy pea flowers
kidney seeds.

Man-fern
has closed its fronds
to the light.

At death's terminus
a palliative cocktail awaits
contorted willow, alder
and oak.

Tree of Heaven, fourteen metres high
watches over a funeral cypress
with ruin on its mind.

The ha-ha wall

(i)   Back in the nineteenth century

On grand English estates, a wall of sunken stone
gave the illusion of garden and grazing fields
as one unbroken landscape

and a ditch dug deep against the outer face
served as a barrier to animals.

Passers-by, enjoying the deception
exclaimed, *Ha-ha.*

Ah ha. A wall that keeps out livestock
can surely keep in people:
to an outsider, merely a low fence,
to an inmate, incarceration.

(ii)   Before the hospital closed

Camouflaged in fading light
a tabby stray stands poised
on a low concrete wall, deciding
if odds are against dropping unharmed
to the trench below, his only access
of entry into Ward 7.

Tomorrow, when day unlocks the doors,
refractory patients will pour outside
to feast their eyes on distant hills
from the yard's best vantage point
before the grass slopes down to a waterless moat
and the ha-ha wall.

(iii)   Today

You can walk some way along it
without fear of falling
now they've filled in the trench.
Tangles of blackberries thrive
and cheeky blackbirds sing:
It's ours, all ours, ha-ha.

Convict wall

2017

I can't agree with Robert Frost who wrote:
Something there is that doesn't love a wall,
that wants it down.

Look what care those masons took,
moulding and firing iron-rich clay into bricks,
patterning colour-tones,

bonding with a paste of shell and sand.
Some have gathered moss, some are painted,
others eroded.

Stand on this gravel track at its southern end.
Run your eye along the vibrant green
of robinia trees casting

dappled shade along the bricks,
arching over to shelter, nurture. These trees
can sense the truth:

this wall was built to protect, not incarcerate.
It offered asylum, encircled a town
within a town.

The Garden

Against a tight girdle
of brickwork, weeds
have burrowed deep
into the down-and-out
soil.

This was once a garden
of fast-growing flowers
planted by a groundskeeper
for the queer folk to watch
from the whey-faced windows.

They would stare
open-mouthed and point
to the sunflowers
growing their big, meaty
heads.

The groundskeeper,
instead of waving, would drag
out dandelion roots
and blow feathery seeds
their way.

Renovating madness

We can do a 60 minute make-over.
Spruce up the hollow-eyed
dormitories and bleached out
bathrooms, just like reality TV.

Let's start by removing the bars
on every window
putting back handles
on all the doors.

Expose the high-beam
hanging posts. Set up speakers
and pipe untroubled music
throughout the place.

Strip the wards
of canvas body holders.
Bulldoze the bed rails
and solitary restraints.

We'll brighten up the brickwork
the shadiest of corners.
Mend all the misery
within.

Shattered

So much broken glass.
One needs to be thick souled
to walk here.

So many shards.
So many empty bathrooms
in which to end
one's sorrows.

Fragments crunch
and chink underfoot

glass confetti tinkling
over the rotting boards
and concrete steps.

It's as if
a bridal party of ghosts
has left a trail.

Glass breakers

Frascati House Ballroom

Imagine
if chandeliers
once lit up this room
masterpieces of glass
that could turn the heads
of dignitaries

and if champagne flutes
fluttered between gloved hands
the vibration of air molecules
exciting the dainty crystal
as heroic tenors reached
their final crescendos.

Now
town bruisers
steal glass vases
from the Garden of Remembrance.
You can see
where they have collided
with the ballroom walls.

These bully boys
thrive in their own
violent opera
with an epic cast
of breaking glass.

Xmas

Scrooge vandals
have carpeted the stairs of C Block
with wreath-green beer labels and
artery-red glass.

They have blocked off the chimneys
glued up the locks
and salted the lawns
where reindeer might rest.

Ding dong merrily on high
in heaven the bells
have stopped
ringing.

The beauty of numbers

On a corner wall of The Barracks
a breakout of numbers
in a sequence of threes and fours
makes no sense
to a maths professor
or an archaeologist –
no one is able to unravel
and decode.

But for someone who saw
the world in fragments
and had a fixation on digits
finding a wall in this hollow square
of a building complex
and pencilling onto the rendered bricks
the first line
1068, 3241, 3128 and 2620
makes perfect sense.

Whether by brilliance or madness
the author of this
mega puzzle of figures
from the soldier's nook on the roof

down into this corner
of the former barracks
perhaps had only one aim—

the beauty of the numbers
themselves.

Statistics

a dissonant word that spits.
At the asylum
it enjoyed great weight.

Hotbeds of numbers
were pulled like hapless worms
from a garden of inmate-intake
by hungry statistician birds

who popped them into tables
to generate facts.
Yet the sum was always less
than its parts – the patients.

Males who'd never married
outnumbered those who had
by five to one.
Females, two to one.
Unknown, one in twenty-one.

How did these statistics help?
How do you measure
loss, fear, loneliness?

Information from the table 'Conjugal Condition, Patients on Register, 30th June, 1916' (Gowlland, p 137).

Why Graffiti?

Graffiti writers are urban shamans
and the streets are our modern day caves.
Crayone

I'm a modern day
calligrapher
writing text
most people can't read.

Writing my name
over and over again
in public places
makes me immortal.

It's a beautiful thing
when I rip the lid
off a spray can
and smell the paint fumes.

When I take on a wall
and do a throwie
I see a new world
in the loudest colours.

It's a kick in the face
to other gangs
who try to take over
my turf.

Love the rush
of quick bombings
the sacrificial speed
over aesthetics.

There's lots of long-faced
walls around here.
I have no choice
but to leave my mark.

Seven ages

The Patchwork Café reminisces (1889 – 2018)

I was a chapel once, crated flat pack
from England, for the nurses' Sunday prayers
and private visits before or after shifts.

I was a school within the asylum grounds.
Watching as heads bent low, as chalk met slate
I offered refuge to children of troubled mothers.

I was a treatment room, a discreet cave
for doctors with new procedures, my doors and drapes
closed to prying eyes. But I saw all.

I was a busy office, a fast-flowing stream
of admissions, a sluggish outflow of the healed
in currents of constant changes, checks and lists.

I was an Industrial Therapy base
filled with apple boxes and baskets
made to occupy long days.

I was a garden shed with a well-worn mattress
a place where couples grasped a moment of pleasure
unseen, in a world deprived of touch.

Now I'm a café. Willow Court has closed
but I am open: to tourists who plumb the past
to locals who nod and smile and look ahead.

New Norfolk

A potted history

Heritage is the glue that binds this place.
Free men from Norfolk Island settled here,
invalid convicts and paupers tasted grace,
the mentally ill were given refuge, care.

Free men from Norfolk Island settled here.
Colonists watched the farms and hopfields flourish.
The mentally ill were given refuge, care
but outlanders mocked the locals, labelled them oddish.

Colonists watched the farms and hopfields flourish,
a peg factory, printery, paper mill sprang up and grew.
Outlanders mocked the locals, labelled them oddish
but folk here fathomed prejudiced points of view.

A peg factory, printery, paper mill sprang up and grew.
Convicts and paupers, long gone, had tasted grace.
Folk here fathom prejudiced points of view
for heritage is the glue that binds this place.

Catharsis

2018

She's drawn to the derelict hospital –
to see it from the outside, looking in.
Fifty years ago, she was inside
looking out, longing for home.

She visits Admissions, now vandalised.
She lived in Ward 4, since demolished
to make way for – what?
Brambles? Tangles of concrete and wire?

She peers through shattered windows
with curtains of Virgin Mary blue.
Upended chairs and smashed cupboards
are all that's left of the dayroom.

Around the silent walls
a sweep of graffiti
boldly speaks its mind.

She remembers the long nights
locked in with fear and despair
the long days, packing pegs in boxes
threading elastic into bloomers

the boredom broken only
by trialling new drugs
group therapy
ECT.

She sees shadows at windows –
the post-natal woman feeding her doll
the doctor's son who wants to suicide –
relives her year's ordeal and lets it rest.

The visits cease.

Timeline

1827	Governor Arthur orders convict invalids be sent to the old Invalid Depot at New Norfolk
1833	Invalid Barracks, including an asylum section, completed
1834	Frascati House built for Colonial Secretary J Burnett
1842	First female ward built
1848	Invalid Barracks approved for insane persons only
1850s	More buildings erected to meet the growing demand
1855	Frascati House purchased by the hospital for the medical superintendent's residence
1859	Gentlemen's Cottage (for fee-paying patients) and a male refractory ward built
1868	Ladies' Cottage built
1883	Royal Commission into management of the hospital
1885	Name change to Hospital for Mental Diseases
1886-9	Construction of Refractory Wards K1, K2 and Olga (Idiots' Ward)
1904	Another Royal Commission. Number of patients housed: 446
1908	Carlton Ward (male maximum security) built
1913	Nurses' Home built
1922	Mental Defectives Act proclaimed
1934	Millbrook Rise Psychopathic Hospital built to aid returning WW 1 veterans and some private patients
1936-9	Wards Derwent, Esperance, Franklin and Glenora built
1937	Name change to Lachlan Park
1940	Administration Building, Hall and Bronte Ward opened
1949	Public Works Committee recommends demolition of many old buildings in Willow Court and a new hospital built on the eastern site across the Lachlan River

1953-9	New Wards 1, 2, 3, 4, 5, 8, 9 and Services Block built on the new site
1964	Myrtle House (Alcheringa) built to house children
1965-73	Demolition of Wards B, H, I, K1 and Services Block at Willow Court
	On western side, new wards constructed: Lyprenny, Lachlan, Allonah. Also Occupational Therapy, Support Program Building, Industrial Therapy
	On eastern side, new wards 6, 7, 10 and 11 occupied
1968	Name change to Royal Derwent Hospital with inclusion of Lachlan Park and Millbrook Rise, and administered by Mental Health Services Commission
	Number of patients peaked at around 1000
1985	The establishment of Willow Court Training Centre for people with intellectual disability
1990s	Progressive moves to community integration and closure of wards
2000	17 November, Willow Court, Australia's oldest asylum operating for 173 years, closed
2001	8 February, the eastern complex of Royal Derwent Hospital closed; remaining residents moved to Millbrook Rise

Adapted from the Australian Heritage Database and the Derwent Valley Council Willow Court Historic Timeline

Bibliography

Dr GM Crabbe, *History of Lachlan Park Hospital*. Manuscript held at LINC, State Library, Hobart

Lawrence Edward Cullen, *Royal Derwent Hospital*, past to present 1936-1978. Manuscript held at LINC, State Library, Hobart

Marion Geyssel, *Royal Derwent Hospital: Willow Court*, a pictorial essay with text by Dr Saxby Pridmore, held at LINC, State Library, Hobart

RW Gowlland, *Troubled Asylum*. Self published, 1981, held at LINC, State Library, Hobart

Roy Porter, *Madness: A social history of madhouses, mad doctors and lunatics* (The History Press Ltd, 2006)

Margaret Reynolds, *Living Politics* (Brisbane: University of Queensland Press, 2007)

Poonkhim Khut, Miranda Morris and Martin Walch, *LivingIn/LivingOut,* an installation, Tasmanian Trades and Labour Council and Mental Health Services, Hobart, Tasmania

The Derwent Valley Gazette. Copies held at New Norfolk Historical Information Centre, New Norfolk, Tasmania

Acknowledgements

The authors thank *Australian Book Review, Cordite, Quadrant, Stylus* and *Communion* for publishing ten of these poems, one in an earlier version.

Very special thanks to: Christiane Conésa-Bostock for her thoughtful compilation of this manuscript,

Mary Blackwood for her insightful foreword,

Megan Schaffner for her valuable suggestions,

Gina Mercer for her expert editing and proofreading,

Sarah Day and Pete Hay for their generous commendations and support,

Ruth Binney and Carol Collins from the New Norfolk Historical Information Centre who, on many occasions, led us to the information we needed,

Barry Lathey from the Derwent Valley Council who provided us with reading material and opened up buildings at Willow Court for us to walk through and find inspiration for our project,

Brett Noble who supplied us with interesting background material,

Volunteers at St Matthews Close Craft Market who answered many of our questions,

Patchwork Café for their delicious meals during our visits to New Norfolk.

Karen Knight has been widely published and anthologised since the early 1960s. She has written four collections of poetry, her most recent, *Postcards from the Asylum* (Pardalote Press, 2008), won the 2005 Dorothy Hewett Flagship Fellowship Award, the 2007 Arts ACT Alec Bolton Award and the 2011 University of Tasmania Prize (Tasmania Book Awards). Karen lives on *Hurdle Farm,* Saltwater River, Tasmania, with her musician husband, Jules, and a menagerie of rescued animals.

Liz McQuilkin has come late to writing. A retired English teacher, she enrolled in a poetry writing course with poet, Gina Mercer, in 2007 and has been widely published since. Her collaboration – with Karen Knight, Christiane Conésa-Bostock, Megan Schaffner and Liz Winfield – in the collection *Of Things Being Various* (Forty Degrees South) won the FAW National Community Award in 2010. Her first solo collection, *The Nonchalant Garden* (Walleah Press), was published in 2014.

Back cover photographs

Liz outside the Invalid Barracks. Photo: Rob McQuilkin.

Karen feeding the stray cats outside the Admission Ward. Photo: Liz McQuilkin.

www.ingramcontent.com/pod-product-compliance
Lightning Source LLC
Chambersburg PA
CBHW021119080526
44587CB00010B/570

* 9 7 8 1 8 7 7 0 1 0 4 1 5 *